The Darling Buds of May

H. E. Bates

Level 3

Retold by Annette Keen
Series Editors: Andy Hopkins and Jocelyn Potter

Pearson Education Limited

Edinburgh Gate, Harlow,

Essex CM20 2JE, England

and Associated Companies throughout the world.

ISBN: 978-1-4058-6769-6

This edition first published by Pearson Education Ltd 2008

1 3 5 7 9 10 8 6 4 2

Text copyright © Pearson Education Ltd 2008

Set in 11/14pt Bembo

Printed in China

SWTC/01

The authors have asserted their moral rights in accordance with the
Copyright Designs and Patents Act 1988

Produced for the Publishers by
Ken Vail Graphic Design

P...

Penguin ...

The pul...

ITV Granada: ...

Every eff...

advance ...

appropri...

For a complete list of the titles available in the Penguin Readers series please write to your local
Pearson Longman office or to: Penguin Readers Marketing Department, Pearson Education,
Edinburgh Gate, Harlow, Essex CM20 2JE

Contents

Introduction

A lot of chickens and four noisy white geese ran away as the children jumped down from the lorry. In the corner of the yard were Pop's three pigs, and there was an old stable for their two horses. The yard was full of old pieces of metal and bits of old cars.

'Home looks nice,' Pop said to Ma. 'It always does, doesn't it?'

They stood looking at the blue and yellow flowers in Ma's little garden near the front door.

'Lovely,' said Ma.

Meet the Larkin family! Pop and Ma Larkin have six bright, happy, hungry children. They live a wonderful life in the country with horses, pigs, chickens and other animals, and they have no worries. Nothing in Pop's life is a problem and everyone is his friend. He never worries about money, work – or the law! Then, one day, when the Larkins come home from the local village, a strange man is waiting for them. He wants to speak to Pop …

H.E. Bates was born in 1905. He was a pilot in the Second World War and at that time he wrote books and short stories about flying and the lives of fighting men. After the war he also wrote about gardening and country life.

Then, in 1958, he decided to write something completely different, and the Larkin family was born. *The Darling Buds of May* was the first of five books about the Larkins. In 1991 the stories were filmed for British television, and were a big success. Catherine Zeta Jones played Mariette, and after this she became a Hollywood star.

H.E. Bates died in January 1974.

Meet the Larkin family.

Chapter 1 The Visitor

Pop★ Larkin bought eight large chocolate ice-creams and gave one to each of his six children. They were all sitting in the back of Pop's blue lorry. He climbed up into the driver's seat and gave one of the ice-creams to Ma.★ The last one was his.

'Are you kids OK in the back?' he shouted as he started the lorry. There was no answer.

'They can't hear you,' said Ma, laughing. 'This lorry is so noisy.'

Pop laughed and shouted again. 'Zinnia and Petunia, Primrose, Victoria, Montgomery, Mariette!' Pop called all their names, but only heard five answering voices.

'Where's Mariette? Isn't she there?'

'I'm here, Pop.'

'That's OK then. Here we go!'

They drove home from the village in the May sunshine, past pink flowering apple trees and strawberry fields.

'Look at that sky, Ma,' said Pop. 'That sky,' he said again, 'is perfick. This day is perfick.'

Pop's favourite word was 'perfect', and in his world almost everything was perfect. But when Pop said it, the word came out as 'perfick'.

Ma laughed. She was a very large woman and she laughed a lot. Pop loved everything about Ma.

'Mariette's quiet today,' he said. 'What's she thinking about?'

'One of her boyfriends, probably.'

Mariette was seventeen, and the oldest of the children. She was a very beautiful girl, with long, black hair and dark eyes. Pop remembered when Ma was seventeen. In those days she looked

★ Pop, Ma: words short for father and mother

1

exactly like Mariette. That was before six children and too many ice-creams made her very fat.

'Shall we stop for a beer?' Pop suggested. 'I've got some in the back of the lorry.'

'No, wait until we get home,' Ma replied. 'We can have one while the food is in the oven.' There was a big bag of fish and chips next to Ma, and the smell was wonderful. It was the Larkins' usual Friday dinner.

'Perfick,' said Pop. 'Are you kids hungry yet?' he shouted to the children. He knew they were. They were always hungry.

Ten minutes later, they were home. The lorry stopped in the yard, outside their house. A lot of chickens and four noisy white geese ran away as the children jumped down from the lorry. In the corner of the yard were Pop's three pigs, and there was an old stable for their two horses. The yard was full of old pieces of metal and bits of old cars.

'Home looks nice,' Pop said to Ma. 'It always does, doesn't it?'

They stood looking at the blue and yellow flowers in Ma's little garden near the front door.

'Lovely,' said Ma. 'Now, let's heat the fish and chips.'

Mariette was still standing by the lorry. There was a strangely worried look on her face.

'Pop,' she said, 'there's a man in the yard. He's over there by the stable, watching us.'

Pop walked across the yard to the stable. Mariette's black horse looked out, over the door. Mariette loved horse riding and she was very good at it. Sometimes she rode in races or jumped at gymkhanas. Pop thought she looked wonderful on a horse. Perfick.

'Hello,' he said to the young man. 'Looking for me?'

The young man was pale, wearing glasses and a dark suit. Under his arm he carried a small black case.

'Mr Sidney Larkin?'

'That's me,' said Pop, laughing. 'What can I do for you? Lovely weather, isn't it?'

'I'm from the tax office.'

Pop looked very surprised.

'Tax office? You're at the wrong house.'

The pale young man opened the black case and took out some papers.

'You haven't sent us your tax form,' he said.

'Nobody asked me to,' replied Pop.

'We sent you a form,' said the young man. 'Like this.'

He held up a sheet of printed paper. Pop looked at it and shook his head.

Ma was walking across the yard from the lorry to the house. She was carrying a box of food under one arm and a bag of fruit under the other. Pop called to her.

'Ma! We didn't have a form like this, did we? This man's from the tax office.'

Ma looked across at them but continued walking.

'I've never seen one like it,' she said. 'Dinner's almost ready.'

The young man looked at Ma, then back at Pop.

'We sent two – maybe three. Here's another. You have to fill in the form ...'

'No time for forms,' said Pop. 'I've got pigs to feed. Chickens to feed. Kids to feed. I haven't had dinner. Nobody's had any dinner.'

Suddenly, the young man wasn't listening. He stood, mouth wide open, watching Mariette. As she walked across the yard, she seemed to him to be the most beautiful girl in the world.

'My oldest daughter, Mister ... Mister ... what's your name?' asked Pop.

'Charlton,' said the young man, as Mariette joined them at the stable. In the bright sunshine, Mr Charlton looked at Mariette. He felt that he was dreaming.

3

'Hello,' she said. Mr Charlton couldn't speak. Mariette tried again. 'Do you like horses?' she asked.

Suddenly, Mr Charlton seemed to wake up.

'I saw you riding at Barfield last Easter,' he said, 'in the third race. You came second.'

Just then, the geese came around the corner of the house.

'We're killing a goose tomorrow,' said Pop. 'We always kill a goose or a few chickens at the weekend. Do you like goose, Mr Charlton?'

Ma, Pop, Mariette – and the man from the tax office

Before Mr Charlton could reply, Ma called from the house.

'Dinner's ready. Come inside, it'll get cold.'

'We've got to go,' said Pop. 'Ma doesn't like waiting.'

The young man tried again. 'Mr Larkin, this form …'

'Did you see me ride at Newchurch, too?' Mariette asked him.

'Yes, I'm sure I did. But Mr Larkin, what about this form?'

'I've had an idea, Mr Charlton. Why don't you come inside and have some dinner with us?'

'I've already eaten, thank you …'

'Well, a cup of tea. Cup of coffee. Bottle of beer. Glass of whisky. You and Mariette can talk some more about riding.'

The young man felt he was spinning. Or maybe the yard was spinning. Before he could refuse, Pop and Mariette pulled him towards the house. Ma was calling a second time.

'Three minutes, or I'll give it to the cats.'

Pop stopped at the door and looked out at his yard – to him, a beautiful place on a beautiful May afternoon.

'Don't you think this place is just perfick, Mr Charlton?'

♦

In the kitchen a radio was playing loudly and in the living room the television was on. There, the family, and Mr Charlton, sat at the crowded table. Mr Charlton was surprised at the amount of food on the table. There were plates of fish and chips, a loaf of bread, a large bowl of fruit, dishes of ice-cream, chocolate cakes, cups of tea and bottles of beer. Mr Charlton was sitting between Ma and Mariette. He had only a cup of tea in front of him.

'Have anything you like,' said Pop. 'How about some chips?'

Mr Charlton thought of the tax form and tried again.

'Mr Larkin, if the form is difficult for you, I can help you fill it in.'

He put the form on the table and took a pen from his pocket.

5

'Full name: Sidney Charles Larkin,' he said. 'Now, how shall we describe your job?'

'Farmer,' said Pop.

Suddenly, Mariette's arm touched Mr Charlton's, and a feeling like electricity ran up his arm. The room started to spin and he couldn't write at all for a few minutes. He took his glasses off, cleaned them and put them on again.

Then, under the table, something moved against his leg. Was it Mariette's leg? He felt weak. But then he saw that it was one of the geese from the yard. The kitchen door was open and two geese were in the room. Nobody seemed to worry about animals coming into the house.

He looked at the form again and asked Pop the next question.

'Mr Larkin, how much money do you earn in a year?'

Mariette turned to look at Mr Charlton. 'Won't you eat something?' she asked. 'Fruit? Ice-cream? Cake? What would you like?'

'Oh, no … thank you. I can't eat fruit – my stomach is quite weak,' said Mr Charlton. 'I usually eat eggs or …'

'I'll boil some eggs for you,' said Mariette, 'and cut you some bread and butter.'

She stood up and went into the kitchen.

'Mr Larkin, your earnings …' Charlie tried again.

Pop laughed. 'I'm lucky if I make five pounds a week. Isn't that right, Ma?'

'Five pounds! I'd like to see five pounds,' Ma said.

'You've got a nice safe job. But are you happy?' Pa asked.

'I don't think you eat enough,' Ma said. 'A week in the country – that's what you need. You spend too much time in that office.'

'What are we eating on Sunday, Ma?' asked Pop. 'Chicken?'

'Just tell me what you want,' said Ma.

Pop thought about it for a minute.

'Goose?' he said. 'Do you like goose or chicken best, Mr Charlton?'

'We'll have both,' Ma decided. 'Goose *and* chicken.'

'Perfick,' said Pop. 'Dinner on Sunday then, Mr Charlton. Two o'clock.'

Mariette arrived back at the table with two brown boiled eggs and some thin pieces of bread and butter.

'Mr Charlton's coming to dinner on Sunday,' said Pop. 'We're having goose and chicken.'

Both geese suddenly walked out of the house and Ma laughed loudly. 'They heard us talking,' she said.

'When you've finished your eggs,' said Pop, 'you should go with Mariette to the woods behind the house. There are birds singing there all day … it's perfick.'

'Oh yes,' said Mariette, smiling. 'Let's do that. It's lovely there and the wild flowers are beautiful.'

Mr Charlton decided to forget the tax form for the rest of the evening. Sunday was soon enough, he thought.

'I'll put a dress on,' said Mariette. 'It's too hot for these trousers.'

She went to change her clothes and Ma started a conversation with Mr Charlton.

'Are you taking your holiday soon?' she asked him. 'Where do you usually go?'

'I don't usually take …' Mr Charlton started.

'You should come strawberry picking with us. Best holiday in the world. And you can earn a lot of money.'

'Perfick,' said Pop. 'Here's Mariette.'

Mr Charlton turned to see Mariette in the doorway. She was wearing a green dress and she looked even more beautiful than before. The room started spinning again.

'Come with me, Mr Charlton,' she said, and held her hand out to him.

'Don't forget about Sunday,' said Pop.

'Are you sure?' asked Mr Charlton.

'Sure? Of course. I'm going to kill the geese now. One goose or two, Ma? Will two be enough? Shall we have three?'

Mr Charlton heard Ma laughing as he and Mariette crossed the yard. Only a few minutes later, they reached the woods. There were hundreds of wild flowers under the trees. Above them, the birds sang loudly.

'It's beautiful, isn't it?' said Mariette. 'If we stand by this gate, we can listen to the birds.'

Mr Charlton couldn't tell one bird from another, but Mariette knew each one by its song.

'That's a blackbird,' she told him, 'and that one's a nightingale.'

Mr Charlton was silent. For the first time in his life, he heard the sound of a nightingale singing against a May evening sky.

'Did you think they only sang at night?' Mariette asked. 'Well, now you know that's not true.'

She laughed and held Mr Charlton's hand. At exactly the same time, he heard the nightingale sing again.

◆

Pop returned to the kitchen after killing three fat geese. He poured himself a glass of beer.

'A few days like this and those strawberries will be ready to pick, Ma.'

Ma was clearing the table. Onto the kitchen fire she threw empty ice-cream boxes, the paper from the fish and chips, and Mr Charlton's tax form.

'I think I'll get some wine for Sunday,' said Pop. He took his beer to the kitchen door and looked out across the yard. A nightingale suddenly sang from the woods.

'Perfick,' said Pop.

Chapter 2 Cards and Cocktails

Mariette and Mr Charlton came back from the woods after an hour. She was carrying some wild flowers and he had two blue bird's eggs in his hand. Pop was feeding the pigs in the yard.

'The pigs look well,' he said. 'I think we'll kill one. Did you hear the nightingales? You're just in time – tea's ready.'

'I thought we just had tea,' said Mr Charlton.

'That was dinner.'

'I really have to catch my bus,' Mr Charlton said. 'The last one leaves at eight o'clock.'

'No, stay for tea,' said Pop. 'Mariette would like that, wouldn't you?' he asked his daughter.

Mariette smiled at Mr Charlton. He looked into her dark eyes and couldn't speak.

'I can take you home in the lorry. Or Mariette can drive you.'

Mr Charlton found his voice again.

'Do you think we could take another look at the tax form? It's really very important,' he said.

'Ma's calling,' replied Pop.

Mr Charlton listened, but he couldn't hear anything.

Mariette walked towards the house. 'I'm going to put these flowers in water,' she said.

Mr Charlton tried again. 'I'll have to write a report for the office. And after that …'

'Beautiful evening, isn't it?' said Pop.

In the kitchen, Ma was cooking steaks. There were piles of cheese and tomato sandwiches on two plates, too.

'How did you like Mr Charlton?' she asked Mariette. 'What was he like?'

'Slow,' she replied. 'He's very shy. He talked about horses most of the time.'

'He mustn't be shy, that won't help. You'll have to find

something more interesting than horses to talk about.'

Then Ma had an idea. 'Put some of my perfume on, Mariette. It's next to the mirror in our bedroom.'

Mariette went upstairs, and Pop and Mr Charlton came in from the yard.

'Strawberry picking on Monday at Benacre, Pop. I heard from Fred Brown,' said Montgomery, the only boy in the family.

Pop was pleased. He loved strawberries.

Ma came in from the kitchen with the plates of steaks and sandwiches. Primrose started pouring tea for everyone. Pop got up from the table and brought a bottle of whisky from the living room.

'Milk?' he asked Ma.

'Please,' said Ma. 'It's just what I need.'

Pop poured whisky into her cup of tea, then into his own cup.

'Some for you, Mr Charlton?' he asked.

'No, no, no. No, really. None for me, thank you.'

Pop filled up his cup with whisky.

'It's good for you,' he said.

Mariette arrived back in the room and sat next to Mr Charlton. Her perfume made his head spin. The flowers from the woods were in the centre of the table. They smelt wonderful, too.

'What's your first name?' Pop asked Mr Charlton.

'Cedric.'

Ma started to laugh.

'Do you play cards, Mr Charlton?' asked Pop.

Mr Charlton shook his head.

'We all play. Mariette can show you.'

'But I really must catch that eight o'clock bus.'

'There isn't an eight o'clock bus now,' said Montgomery. 'They stopped it last year.'

Mr Charlton got up from the table.

10

'Then I must start walking,' he said. 'It's eight miles to town.'

'Why don't you stay for the night?' asked Pop. 'We've got plenty of room.'

'Oh, no, I really must …'

'But tomorrow's Saturday – you don't have to go to the office on Saturday, do you?' said Mariette. 'Please stay – we can go riding tomorrow. It's going to be lovely weather again.'

Mariette's dark eyes and her perfume made Mr Charlton's head spin again. He sat down.

'But I haven't got any pyjamas with me.'

'You're about the same size as me – I'll lend you a pair of my pyjamas,' said Mariette.

Primrose poured Mr Charlton another cup of tea, and Pop filled it up with whisky.

'You could come strawberry picking with us,' he suggested.

Mr Charlton suddenly remembered the tax form. But before he could speak, the television programme changed. Montgomery turned the sound up and everyone at the table turned to look at the television.

A voice in Mr Charlton's head shouted, 'Tax form! Tax form!' Mariette took his hand in hers. 'Tax form!'

'Another sandwich?' asked Ma.

'Tax form,' he thought. But the voice in his head was getting softer and Mariette's perfume was getting stronger.

◆

At half past ten, Pop, Ma and Mariette were still trying to teach Mr Charlton how to play cards. It was impossible. He couldn't understand the game they played. He didn't know the language they used. He couldn't add up the cards.

'You've got to use your head in this game,' said Pop.

Mr Charlton was trying very hard to use his head, but it seemed to be asleep. Pop explained the rules of the card game to him

11

again, but it was no good. He understood numbers in the office, but these numbers were different. He finished his second beer of the evening.

'I'll mix a cocktail,' said Pop. 'Mr Charlton, you'd like a cocktail, wouldn't you? I'll find a special one to mix.'

Pop picked up a book, *A Guide to Better Drinking*, and started looking through it.

'Here's one we haven't tried,' he said. 'It's called the Rolls Royce.'

'That sounds nice,' said Ma.

Pop mixed the cocktail from a lot of different bottles. Then he poured it into four glasses. Pop and Ma drank. Mariette drank.

'Perfick,' said Pop.

'Lovely,' said Ma and Mariette together.

Mr Charlton drank. The cocktail was very strong. It burned his tongue. Then it burned his stomach. Hot tears came into his eyes. He couldn't speak.

'Come strawberry picking with us on Monday,' said Mariette. 'You can eat as many as you like, and you earn good money.'

Mr Charlton tried to speak. He wanted to say something about the office, and work. He wanted to say that he couldn't take a holiday next week. But the Rolls Royce was still burning his mouth and he couldn't say anything.

'Another cocktail?' asked Pop, filling Mr Charlton's glass again. 'Ma, how about a nice chicken sandwich with this?'

Something about that idea amused Mr Charlton. He laughed, and this pleased Pop very much.

'You're just like one of the family,' Pop said. 'Everything is perfick!'

Ma agreed. 'We feel we've known you for years,' she said.

Mariette moved her chair closer to Mr Charlton's.

'Mariette, what's that perfume you're wearing?' he asked her.

'It's called Pink Roses,' she said. 'Do you like it?'

'Like it? Like it? I love it!' he said, and he drank the rest of his Rolls Royce.

Pop mixed another cocktail, a last one before they went to bed. This one was called the Driver. There was a lot of whisky in it, some red wine and very little fruit juice.

'Must have a Driver with a Rolls Royce,' said Pop as he filled Mr Charlton's glass with the new cocktail.

Mr Charlton drank it too quickly, then tried to stand up. This was difficult, but Mariette helped him.

'Can't thank you enough,' he said to Pop and Ma. 'Can never thank you.'

Mariette took him with her to find the pyjamas. Then she made a bed for him in a room nobody used.

Pop and Ma turned out the lights and went upstairs to their bedroom.

'What do you think about Mr Charlton?' Pop asked Ma.

'He'll be OK,' she replied. 'He just needs a bit more time.'

Chapter 3 The Rolls Royce

Mr Charlton woke late, with a terrible headache. At first, he thought there was a storm outside. He could hear a lot of noises. He listened again. The noises were in his head.

He was wearing Mariette's pyjamas, blue with pink flowers on them. He couldn't remember putting the pyjamas on the night before. He got out of bed slowly, because of his headache, and put his trousers on over the pyjamas.

Ma was in the kitchen, cooking breakfast.

'One egg or two?' she asked him. 'Two eggs or three?' She put a cup of tea in front of him. 'Mariette waited for you, but now she's gone riding.'

Mr Charlton didn't feel well. He shut his eyes, but that was a mistake. The room started to spin, so he opened his eyes again. He saw Pop coming into the kitchen.

'How's my friend? Sleep well?' Pop shouted.

Mr Charlton put a hand to his head. He was surprised to find it was still there. The sound of Pop's voice crashed around inside it.

'I don't think Mr Charlton's feeling very well,' said Ma.

'I should go home,' said Mr Charlton in a very small voice.

'You need a Larkin Special,' said Pop. 'Then you'll be fine.'

The kitchen door opened again, and Mariette came in.

'Hello, bright eyes,' she said. 'How are you today?'

'Not too well. I'll probably get the bus home this morning.'

'You worry too much,' said Pop. He put an arm round Mr Charlton's shoulder. 'I don't feel right calling you Cedric. Can we call you Charley?' he said. 'Is that OK?'

Mr Charlton looked up − slowly, because of his headache.

'Yes,' he said softly. 'That's OK.'

'Don't go home,' said Mariette. 'It's a lovely day. We can walk to the river and have a look at our boat.'

'You've got a boat?' Thoughts of the tax office came into Mr Charlton's head, and then he remembered the form. 'Mrs Larkin, do you know what happened to that tax form? The one I brought here yesterday?'

Pop put a glass on the table, in front of Mr Charlton. The drink in it was the colour of blood.

'A Larkin Special,' said Pop. 'Drink it, and you'll soon be perfick again.'

Mr Charlton looked at it. His head ached. His stomach hurt. He looked up at Mariette, and she smiled at him. He lifted the glass and drank until it was empty. Slowly he started to feel better.

'You're not really going home, are you?' Mariette asked him. 'It's wonderful in the woods today. There are so many more flowers since yesterday. Lots of little buds have opened today. Please stay.'

Mr Charlton thought again of his office. He remembered the

noise of typing. He remembered the ringing telephones and the pile of papers ... It wasn't a pleasant thought.

'Well, if it's not a problem ...' he said, looking at Ma.

'Problem? We love having you. We want you to stay.'

'You just need some fresh air,' added Mariette.

Mr Charlton went to the kitchen door and stood in the sun. The sky was bright blue. Across the yard he could see the flowers at the start of the woods. Somewhere close, a bird was calling.

'How do you feel now?' asked Mariette.

Mr Charlton smiled. 'A little more perfick than I was.'

♦

The next morning, Ma was busy in the kitchen cooking the geese for Sunday lunch. Pop was out somewhere and the Larkin children were feeding the animals in the yard.

'Let's eat outside,' said Ma. 'It's so hot today.'

Mariette and Mr Charlton carried the table into the garden and put it under a large tree. They put a large white cloth on it and then they brought knives, forks and glasses from the kitchen.

At half past twelve, Pop surprised everybody by driving into the yard in a large, black, shiny Rolls Royce.

'All in!' he shouted. 'Everybody in! If you want a ride, get in!'

The Larkins and Mr Charlton climbed into the beautiful car.

'I've wanted to buy this for a long time. Now it's ours!' said Pop happily.

'It's wonderful,' said Ma, laughing. 'Wait until they see this in the village. They'll put the price of fish and chips up.'

Pop started the car and drove slowly round and round the yard. The car was silent. The passengers were silent.

'Perfick, isn't it? Just perfick.'

'It's like riding on air,' said Mariette.

'Ma, you should be wearing your best hat,' said Montgomery, and everyone laughed.

'Look at that pipe in the back, Ma,' Pop shouted, over his shoulder. 'You can talk into that and give me orders. I can hear what you say. Try it.'

Ma was a little afraid of trying it. Then she suddenly remembered that the geese were cooking in the oven.

'Home, driver!' she said.

Pop drove round the yard again and stopped the car by the front door. Ma hurried into the kitchen.

The rest of the family climbed out of the Rolls Royce. Mariette took Mr Charlton's hand. They went together to sit at the table under the tree.

'Charley,' called Pop. 'Can you do something for me? Get some ice for the wine?'

'Pop, we've got a visitor,' said Montgomery. 'It looks like the Brigadier.'

A tall, thin man with white hair and a moustache was coming towards them. Pop got out of the car and waved to him. The Brigadier was one of the Larkins' neighbours, and Pop liked him very much. They shook hands and the Brigadier looked at the Rolls Royce with surprise.

'It's not yours, Larkin, is it?' he asked.

'Yes, it's mine,' said Pop, proudly. 'I got it for a good price. It was cheaper than I thought. I knew the family would love it.'

'A car like this can use a lot of petrol. Won't it be very expensive?'

'Maybe, maybe not. I don't know yet. But if it is, I'll sell it.'

Pop bought a lot of things and in the end he sold most of them again. He didn't usually lose any money.

'Excellent,' said the Brigadier. 'Excellent car.'

'Come in, come in!' said Pop. 'Ma will be happy to see you.'

They went together into the kitchen. The smell of the geese cooking was wonderful.

'Hello, Brigadier. How's your sister today?' she asked.

16

'Visiting friends,' the Brigadier replied.

He lived with his sister. Pop often thought she didn't give him enough food. The Brigadier was much too thin, in his opinion.

'Stay for lunch,' he said. 'Ma's cooked plenty – you'll be welcome. Don't eat on your own.'

The Brigadier was pleased. 'Very kind of you, Larkin. Very kind,' he said. 'There's something I wanted to ask you. I've got a bit of a problem.'

Pop took the Brigadier into the living room and poured them both a whisky. The Brigadier looked worried and Pop wanted to help.

'What's the problem? Women?' he asked.

The Brigadier looked very surprised.

'Not as bad as that, but bad enough, Larkin,' he said.

'Ask me anything. I'll help if I can. '

'It's about the gymkhana,' said the Brigadier. 'We can't have the field we usually use. The farmer refuses to lend it to us this year and we can't find another one.'

The gymkhana was in two weeks' time.

'Oh, that's no problem,' said Pop. 'You can use my field, the one at the back of the house. I'll cut the grass this week and then it'll be perfick.'

The Brigadier was very grateful.

'Can't thank you enough, Larkin,' he said. 'We can have the gymkhana now, thanks to you.'

Pop gave him another glass of whisky and went to the kitchen for ice. Ma was looking out of the window at Mariette and Mr Charlton. They were sitting at opposite ends of the table under the tree, reading the Sunday newspapers.

'They're not even sitting together,' she said. 'What's wrong with them?'

'Perhaps this afternoon will be better. They're going to take the boat up the river.'

17

Everyone agreed that the goose tasted wonderful.

Lunch was soon ready, and everyone helped carry the food outside. The Brigadier was surprised when plate after plate and dish after dish was put onto the table. He hoped the table was strong enough for the weight of so much food.

'Charley, if you want to help, you can pour the wine,' Pop said.

Pop cut the meat and Ma passed the dishes of vegetables round the table. Everyone agreed that the goose tasted wonderful. Pop told them all about the problem with the gymkhana, and his offer of the field.

Mariette was happy and excited. She got up, ran round the table and kissed Pop.

'Thank you, Pop! You're a lovely, lovely man!'

'It was the Brigadier's idea,' said Pop.

So Mariette kissed the Brigadier. Then, because she was so happy, she kissed Mr Charlton. His face went very red. Everyone laughed, and Mariette kissed him again.

'There'll be things to plan for the gymkhana,' said the Brigadier. 'I'm sure Edith will come to see you about it.'

Pop liked Edith Pilchester. He could always have a joke with Edith.

'How about fireworks after the gymkhana? I'll buy them,' said Pop. 'They'll make a good end to the day. I'll ask Edith about it when I see her.'

After lunch, the younger children went off to play. The Brigadier fell asleep at the table. Soon, Ma was also asleep.

'Look at that, Charley,' said Pop, pointing at the clear blue sky above them. 'That's something special for you to remember. I don't know how you can work in an office, with that outside your window.'

Mr Charlton was beginning to have the same idea.

'We're going for a walk now,' said Mariette. She stood up and took Mr Charlton's hand.

'Are you going on the boat?' asked Pop.

'Maybe, if we get that far.'

'Perfick, anywhere you go.'

Mariette and Mr Charlton crossed the garden to the big field behind the house. All around them the perfume of wild flowers hung on the warm air.

Suddenly, Mariette took off her shoes and started running towards the river. Mr Charlton thought again how wonderful she looked. He ran after her.

Chapter 4 Picking Strawberries

That evening, Pop talked to Mr Charlton about his job.

'Ma doesn't think you look very well,' he said. 'You should call your office, Tell them you're sick.'

Later, Mariette said something similar to him.

'If you take a week off work, you can come strawberry picking. And then you can stay next Saturday and Sunday too.'

Then she kissed him and it started to seem like a good idea.

Next morning, Mr Charlton came down to a big breakfast. Pop was already at the table and Ma was cooking more eggs for the children.

'It's going to be a perfick day,' Pop said. 'The birds started singing at four o'clock.'

'I don't know what to tell them at the office,' Mr Charlton said. 'Honestly, there's nothing wrong with me. I feel fine – better than usual.'

'Then you must make something up, mustn't you? How about back ache?'

'But I never have back ache.'

'You will tonight, after your first day picking strawberries,' laughed Pop. 'You'll have very bad back ache. So if you tell them that at the office, it'll be true.'

So at eight o'clock, Mr Charlton was sitting in the back of the lorry with Mariette and the other children. It wasn't long before they were all singing.

Only Mr Charlton was quiet. He was not used to singing in front of other people. He was also thinking that the large breakfast was not a very good idea. It wasn't a smooth ride in the lorry and he was starting to feel sick.

Luckily, it was a short journey to the strawberry fields. It was already hot and there wasn't a cloud in the sky. In the open fields there was nowhere to get out of the sun, just miles of strawberry plants. Mr Charlton noticed a small tent at the side of the field. He saw the shadows inside. It looked very nice and quiet.

Out in the fields there were already twenty or thirty women picking fruit. Mariette took his hand.

'Stay near me,' she said. 'You can eat all the strawberries you like. You'll probably get tired of that soon.'

Mr Charlton didn't feel like eating any strawberries at all. Now and then he looked up to see Mariette biting into one. The rest of the Larkin children seemed to be eating them all the time.

He soon found that he was very slow. Mariette could fill three boxes to one of his.

'You're not very fast, are you?' she asked him. 'Don't you feel very well? Let's go to the tent and weigh the boxes. They all have to be checked there.'

Mr Charlton was happy with this suggestion. He thought he would enjoy being in the tent more than in the hot sun.

Pop was there at the same time, with his first boxes of strawberries. He introduced Mr Jennings. Mr Jennings was checking and weighing the boxes.

'This is Charley, a friend of ours. He works in a tax office.'

Mr Jennings was interested. Not many strawberry pickers knew anything about paperwork. 'You're just the man I'm looking for,' he said. 'How about sitting here and weighing the boxes for me? I've got a hundred other things to do.'

Mr Jennings explained everything to Mr Charlton.

'You just have to write people's names in the book with the weight of their boxes. Then we can pay them at the end of the day. I'll come back in an hour to see you.'

Pop laughed and shook Mr Charlton's hand.

'There you are, Charley! I've got you a better job already. Well, I'm going into town now to see a man about a bit of business. See you at about five o'clock.'

The weighing job seemed perfectly easy to Mr Charlton.

21

Sitting down in the tent, he suddenly felt more comfortable. It was almost like being back at the office.

'Are you feeling better now?' asked Mariette, kissing the top of his head.

'Much better.'

'You see, I told you. You just need some fresh air and good food. See you later – and don't talk to the other women.'

It was soon very busy in the little tent, with women bringing in lots of boxes for weighing. The Larkins arrived with their boxes. Soon after they left, a pretty, fair-haired girl of about Mariette's age came in. She was wearing tight black jeans and a very tight black shirt.

'Pauline Jackson,' she said. 'Twenty boxes. Are you new here? I haven't seen you before.'

'I'm on holiday,' Mr Charlton explained.

'That's nice,' she said. 'Is your name really Cedric? That's what they're saying out there.'

Mr Charlton's face turned red.

'Oh no,' he said. 'No, I'm Charley. That's my name. Ask any of the Larkin family. Ask Mariette.'

'Oh, you know her, do you?'

Pauline Jackson sat on the corner of the desk and bit into a large red strawberry.

'Don't you like these?' she asked, moving closer to Mr Charlton. 'Wouldn't you like one?'

Nervously, he turned over the pages of the book.

Just then, Mariette came into the tent with her boxes. Pauline Jackson got off the desk and started to walk towards the entrance.

'Well, see you later, Charley,' she said as she walked straight past Mariette and out into the fields.

Mariette put her boxes down on the table with a crash.

'She isn't a nice girl, Charley. Don't get too friendly with her!'

Mr Charlton saw two of the older women coming towards the tent.

'Wait until they've gone, Mariette. I want to talk to you …'

'She makes me so angry!'

'Please wait just a minute …'

'It's too hot here – I'm going to the woods. I'll be there if you want me.'

By the middle of the afternoon, it was even hotter. Mr Charlton was adding up the total amount of strawberries picked until that time. He knew how much Mr Jennings paid the women for the fruit. Just as he was thinking about the tax on all that money, Pauline Jackson arrived back in the tent.

'What time do you finish work?' she asked him.

'I … I'm not really sure, Miss Jackson.'

'You don't have to call me that. You can call me Pauline,' she said, and moved closer to Mr Charlton. 'I'm going to finish soon. Then I think I'll go for a swim at the pool. You could come with me,' she suggested.

He moved his chair back a little.

'Oh, well, no … I need to get some clothes from my room in Fordington,' he said.

'That's OK, I can wait.'

'But I really don't know what time … or … '

'There's no hurry. Just say when,' she said, and she walked out of the tent back to the strawberry fields.

Two other women arrived in the tent as Pauline Jackson was leaving. Mr Charlton took their boxes, weighed them, and wrote the amounts in the book.

Just then, they heard the sound of shouting outside in the field and they all hurried to the door of the tent. In the middle of the field, two girls were fighting like wild cats. A circle of women was watching the fight, and the two girls in the centre were screaming and kicking. Suddenly, the circle opened a little. Mr Charlton saw that the wild cats were Mariette and Pauline Jackson. At first, he thought there was blood on their arms and faces. Then he realized it was strawberry juice.

He was worried about Mariette, and felt a little sick. Should he stop the fight before she *did* get hurt?

'I must stop them!' he said to the woman next to him. 'Why are they fighting?'

'Don't you know?' the woman replied. 'It's *you*. They're fighting about *you*.'

Mr Charlton couldn't believe it. On the journey home in the lorry, he looked at Mariette and smiled. She had red strawberry juice in her hair from the fight, and he felt very proud of her.

Back home, Pop poured a beer for Mr Charlton and one for himself. Ma was cooking dinner and Mariette was changing her clothes.

'So how was the first day, Charley?' Pop said. 'Everything all right. No back ache?'

'No back ache,' Mr Charlton said. 'Everything was fine.'

'Perfick,' Pop said. 'How did you do, Ma? Good picking?'

'I earned fourteen pounds.' Ma said.

'I was thinking,' said Mr Charlton. 'Do the strawberry pickers pay tax on the money that they're paid?'

'Pay tax?' said Pop. 'What do *you* think?'

Mr Charlton thought they probably didn't. Then Mariette arrived in the room wearing her green dress. He stopped worrying about the strawberry tax.

'You've got an hour before dinner,' said Pop. 'Enough time to take Mariette for a walk to the river.'

Mr Charlton agreed and went to find Mariette.

In the kitchen, Ma heard the conversation and decided not to hurry with the cooking. She watched the young people walk across the yard and into the field. The grass and wild flowers were so tall that soon she couldn't see them.

The grass and wild flowers were so tall that soon she couldn't see them.

Chapter 5 Miss Pilchester and the Kiss

When Pop got home the next evening, he found Miss Pilchester in the yard.

'It's all just terrible,' she said.

Pop didn't ask her what was terrible. To Miss Pilchester, most things in life were terrible. She lived alone and had no help with her house or garden. She kept chickens for their eggs but nobody helped her with those, either. She didn't have enough money for a car. It was all just terrible.

Miss Pilchester was very good at helping to plan activities in the village. The gymkhana was one of the things she liked planning most of all.

'It's hot again, isn't it?' said Pop. 'Another lovely day.'

'Terrible,' replied Miss Pilchester. 'Just terrible.' She was wearing a thick winter skirt and jacket.

They went together to look at Pop's field. The grass was short now, with the tall white and yellow flowers growing only around the outside.

'It's a wonderful field, Larkin. It's just what we need. You've saved this year's gymkhana.'

In her mind Miss Pilchester could already see the field on gymkhana day. She imagined the small tent for the judges, the beer tents, the horses, and the villagers watching the riding.

'I like to help if I can,' said Pop, laughing.

'What about the car park? That's always a problem.'

'You can use the small field next to this one. It's simple!' said Pop, laughing again.

Miss Pilchester laughed, too. She liked Pop because he was always happy and friendly. He made her feel happy, too. Sometimes, Pop kissed her. She still remembered a kiss at a village dance, a year or more ago. She liked to think about it when everything was just terrible. That was quite often.

'The field is all yours. You can come and go just as you like, at any time,' said Pop.

'We just want a fine day now,' she said. 'If it rains, it'll be just terrible.'

'That's one thing I can't help with!' Pop replied, laughing. 'But, talking of water, how about a little drink? I suddenly feel quite thirsty.'

They walked together to the house. Ma was in the kitchen cutting meat.

'Doctor Leagrave's here,' said Ma. 'He's waiting to see you.'

'Good. We'll ask him to have a look at Charley.'

Pop took Miss Pilchester into the living room and shook hands with the doctor. As usual in the Larkin house, the television was on. The programme was about a man called Wagner and his music.

Pop didn't understand any of it and he didn't like the music, either. He turned the sound down but he didn't turn the television off. The people in the programme opened and closed their mouths silently.

'Were you visiting patients today?' Miss Pilchester asked the doctor. 'It's a very hot day for that. Terrible.'

'No, not this afternoon,' said the Doctor.

Doctor Leagrave knew there was always a glass of whisky for him at the Larkin house. It wasn't unusual for him to stop there on his way home.

Pop was already handing him a whisky.

'Now, Miss Pilchester,' he said. 'Edith. What would you like? Whisky? Or I can mix you a cocktail?'

Miss Pilchester liked it when Pop called her Edith. She smiled softly and asked for a whisky.

'Cocktails are just terrible,' she said.

Pop thought about mixing himself a Rolls Royce. Or perhaps he should have a Driver? It was difficult to choose. Finally, he decided on a beer.

'A friend of Mariette's is staying with us, Doctor. He's got a bad back. Do you think you could have a look at him?' he asked the doctor.

Mr Charlton came home soon after his second day in the strawberry fields. His face was red from the sun and he was very hungry. He couldn't remember feeling so hungry before. He looked very healthy and he felt better than ever.

Pop took Mr Charlton and the doctor upstairs. He showed them into Mariette's bedroom, without knocking first. Luckily, Mariette wasn't there.

Mr Charlton took off his shirt and lay face down on the bed. All around him was the smell of the Pink Roses perfume that Mariette wore.

Doctor Leagrave pressed his fingers into Mr Charlton's back.

'Does this hurt?' he asked. 'Any pain here?'

Mr Charlton didn't have back ache. There was nothing wrong with him, but he didn't tell that to Doctor Leagrave.

'Not really,' he said.

'It probably comes and goes,' said the Doctor.

'Something like that,' Mr Charlton agreed.

'Well, it's a good idea to stay off work for a week or two.'

Mr Charlton was very pleased with this. He was having a wonderful time in the strawberry fields, and he was earning good money. He didn't want to go back to work.

◆

Some time later, after Miss Pilchester's third whisky, Pop offered to drive her home.

'We've got a Rolls Royce now,' he said.

'Yes, I saw it in the yard. It's a wonderful car.'

Pop spent some time showing Miss Pilchester why the Rolls Royce was so special.

'You can sit in the back, if you like,' he said. 'You'll feel like the Queen. You can speak into this pipe and give me orders.'

'No, thanks,' said Miss Pilchester. 'I want to sit in the front with you.'

At first, Pop drove very fast. He wanted Miss Pilchester to hear how quiet the car was. But her house was less than a mile away and she didn't want to arrive there too quickly.

'I don't like to drive so fast. Slow down,' she said.

So Pop drove her home slowly, with one hand. The other hand was on her knee. He preferred Ma's larger knees, but Miss Pilchester seemed to enjoy it.

When they reached her house, Miss Pilchester asked Pop to come in for a drink. The little house was dark, dirty and very untidy, and Pop couldn't find a seat. There were dirty cups and dishes everywhere. Miss Pilchester picked up magazines, a newspaper, a pair of socks, a bowl of brown eggs and a book about chickens.

Finally, there was an empty chair for Pop to sit on.

She went to the kitchen to get him a drink. The bottle of whisky was nearly empty. She knew there wasn't another one in the house. Then she had a good idea. She put a little water into the bottle. Slowly she mixed the whisky and water together, then she emptied the bottle into two glasses.

Pop was looking around the room when she came back.

'No television?' he asked. He couldn't imagine a house without a television.

'Too expensive,' she replied. 'It's just terrible.'

She gave Pop one of the glasses and thanked him again for being so nice about the field. Pop drank his whisky. He knew immediately that there was water in it.

'Well, Edith. I must go. I've got lots of things to do before bedtime,' said Pop, and he stood up.

'Oh, must you go?' asked Miss Pilchester. She stood up, too. 'You've been wonderful.'

Pop put his arms around her and gave her a kiss. Miss Pilchester enjoyed the kiss very much.

'Another one?' asked Pop.

'Yes, please.'

'Perfick.'

After the second kiss, Miss Pilchester felt wonderful. She forgot to say that anything was terrible.

A few minutes later, Pop drove away in the Rolls Royce, and she waved to him from her gate.

'See you soon!' she called.

♦

When Pop arrived home, Ma was sitting outside the kitchen door. She was enjoying a glass of beer. It was still hot in the evening air, and just starting to get dark. Pop went into the house and poured himself a glass of beer. Then he joined Ma outside.

29

'Where's Charley?' he asked.

'He's gone to the post office with Mariette. He wanted to post a letter.'

'A letter? Why is he writing letters?'

Pop couldn't understand anybody writing a letter. He never wrote letters. None of the Larkins wrote letters.

'It was a letter to the tax office,' said Ma.

'Not about us?' asked Pop.

'No, of course not. He told them about the doctor's visit. I think he's going to stay for another week or two.'

'Perfick,' said Pop.

'Well,' said Ma, 'did you kiss her?'

'Of course I did.'

'Good. I thought you would. She'll sleep much better now,' said Ma. She was not at all worried. 'What was it like?' asked Ma.

Pop thought for a minute.

'It was a bit like kissing a horse,' he said. 'She's got a small moustache – but it's quite soft!'

Ma laughed.

Pop looked up at the stars in the night sky. A few drops of rain fell. Pop started to tell Ma about Miss Pilchester's dark little house, and how untidy and dirty it was.

'And no television,' he added.

They sat in silence for a few minutes until at last Ma said, 'Well, I'm waiting.'

'What for?'

'You kissed Edith. Isn't it about time you kissed *me*?'

Pop thought she was quite right.

A few fresh, warm drops of rain fell onto their faces, but to Pop and Ma it didn't matter at all.

Chapter 6 The Gymkhana

On the day of the gymkhana Mr Charlton was up at half past four. The morning was cloudy. Pop thought it would be fine by midday. He was already feeding the animals when Mr Charlton came down for breakfast. Mariette cooked eggs, tomatoes and potatoes for him. She looked pretty and fresh in dark green trousers and a pale yellow shirt. She was almost too excited to eat anything. Ma was staying in bed for another hour. She wanted to be ready for a long day.

As Mr Charlton took a fifth piece of bread and covered it thickly with butter, Pop smiled. The young man was looking healthier already.

'Are you two going to feed the donkeys?' he asked. 'I've got a thousand things to do, and Miss Pilchester will be here by six.'

'Oh! Those sweet donkeys. Yes, of course we will,' said Mariette.

The donkeys were new to the Larkin family. Pop wanted to add a donkey race to the gymkhana.

'To make the day more interesting,' he explained.

The four animals were now living happily in the stables with Mariette's horse.

Pop's offer of fireworks was not popular with the people planning the gymkhana. They were worried about frightening the horses. Pop understood this. 'But I think it's a pity,' he told Ma. He planned to introduce a few private little jokes of his own and nobody except Pop knew about them.

Then he had another idea – a cocktail party after the gymkhana. It was the perfick answer. Ma agreed.

'But not more than about thirty people,' she said.

'What time is the cocktail party, Pop?' Mr Charlton asked.

Pop was very pleased that Mr Charlton was now calling him Pop and not Mr Larkin.

31

'Ma thinks eight o'clock is the perfick time.'

'What a day,' said Mariette. 'All this and cocktails too. I've never been to a cocktail party.'

'Neither have I,' replied Pop. 'Neither has Ma.'

'What do people drink at cocktail parties?' Mariette asked.

'Cocktails!' laughed Mr Charlton, and Mariette hit him lightly on the shoulder.

'Not at our party,' said Pop. 'Have you forgotten?'

Both Mariette and Mr Charlton were too excited to remember discussing the food and drink a few days before. At that time Pop wanted to mix some of the stronger cocktails from his *Guide to Better Drinking*. There was one with a French name that he couldn't say.

'In English it means My Darling,' said Mr Charlton.

Pop liked the sound of that.

'I don't think it's a good idea,' said Mr Charlton. 'It will be much too strong for some people,' he said.

Pop thought again.

'Let's have champagne!' he suggested.

Both Ma and Mariette loved the idea.

'Something nice always happens when you drink champagne,' said Mariette, and she smiled softly at Mr Charlton. He smiled back at her and Pop saw their secret smiles. He almost said something, but decided to keep quiet.

There was then the question of food. Pop and Ma didn't know what people ate at cocktail parties. Mr Charlton was asked again for his opinion.

'You need cheese and little sandwiches. Things that people can just eat with their fingers,' he said.

Ma didn't think that was enough for anybody.

Pop wanted chips, but Mr Charlton said no to that.

Mariette thought of cold fish on small squares of bread. Mr Charlton suggested cold chicken and small, sweet tomatoes.

So the decisions about food and drink were already made.

It was half past five before Mariette and Mr Charlton got up from the breakfast table. They went across the yard to feed the four little donkeys in the stable. There were three more donkeys arriving later in the morning.

As soon as they were in the stable, Mr Charlton put his arms around Mariette. Then he kissed her.

Mariette laughed. 'I couldn't wait for this first, loveliest kiss of the day,' she said.

Mr Charlton agreed.

As they kissed a second time, the donkeys moved quietly behind them.

'There's a first time for everything,' said Mariette, laughing. 'This is the first time I've kissed anyone in a stable!'

Mr Charlton was starting to use his head, after three weeks living with the Larkins and days in the strawberry fields.

'Just wait until the cocktail party,' he said.

♦

At half past ten, Miss Pilchester arrived in a taxi. She was four hours later than planned, and she was nervous and worried at the same time. She was carrying lists of the horses and the names of their riders for the judges, a pair of boots, another jacket, her lunch and some books. As she got out of the taxi she dropped most of these things.

The Brigadier helped her pick them up. Five minutes later, Miss Pilchester was busy checking everything.

'Where are the microphones? Is the food tent ready? And what about the donkeys — are they here yet?' she asked.

The Brigadier answered her questions calmly.

'Edith, everything is fine. The microphones are ready, the tents are ready, and some of the donkeys have been here all night. There's nothing to worry about.'

Suddenly, she remembered something that she *did* need to worry about. The chief judge was arriving by train. He needed a car to bring him to the gymkhana field.

Just then, Ma came out of the house.

'I've got a very rude man on the phone. He's waiting at the station for you, Edith.'

'We must do something quickly! Who can meet him? *I* can't go. There are too many things for me to do here. This is just terrible!'

The judge was a very important man and Miss Pilchester didn't want him to wait too long at the station.

'Edith, it's not a problem. Mariette and Mr Charlton can go in the car,' said Pop. 'They need to get more champagne.'

'Champagne? What champagne? Who ordered champagne?'

'I did.'

'Not for this show?'

'No, for the cocktail party this evening. You were invited – don't you remember?' asked Pop. 'I couldn't have the fireworks, so we decided to have a cocktail party.'

'You will promise me, won't you – no fireworks?' asked Miss Pilchester.

'Of course, I said so.'

'Not one?'

'No fireworks,' said Pop. But he didn't promise.

♦

Soon after twelve o'clock, Pop went to the beer tent. Some of the local people were there, and also the important judge. Pop said hello to everyone, but not all the men replied. He knew why – they weren't invited to the cocktail party.

Pop got himself a glass of beer and went to talk to Sir George Bluff-Gore. Sir George owned Bluff Court, the largest house in the area. It was three hundred years old, with sixty rooms. A lot of work was needed on it, but repairs were too expensive. Sir George

'No fireworks,' said Pop. But he didn't promise.

and Lady Rose lived in a little house in the gardens and didn't use Bluff Court at all.

'It's very nice of you to invite us to your party, Larkin,' he said. 'We don't get out much.'

Pop liked Sir George. He remembered meeting Lady Rose once or twice and then he suddenly thought of their daughter, Rosemary.

'Bring your daughter tonight, she's very welcome.'

'She lives in London now,' said Sir George. 'She doesn't want the country life. It broke her mother's heart. She won't come back here to live, only to visit. She's at college, taking a course in art.'

Then Pop surprised him with a sudden question.

'When are you going to sell Bluff Court, Sir George?'

Sir George went white. He didn't want to sell his family home. It was much too large, needed a lot of gardeners and cleaners and was never, ever warm in winter. His wife didn't like it and Rosemary didn't want to live there. But Sir George didn't want to sell it.

'Larkin – hundreds of years of my family's history is there. I can't sell Bluff Court. Why did you ask me?'

'Because you don't live in it!' laughed Pop. 'You use your television, don't you? You don't keep it switched off? It's the same thing!'

This was something Sir George didn't really understand. He didn't have a television.

'Were you thinking of buying it, then?' he asked Pop.

'Of course! That's why I asked you.'

'So you'd like to live there?'

Pop took a long drink from his glass of beer.

'Live there? No! I'd like to pull the place down!' he said, laughing.

Sir George's face went even whiter. He couldn't speak at all.

'I'll give you a good price. And it won't be a cheque,

either. Think about it,' said Pop, and he walked out of the beer tent into the bright sunshine.

Mariette was on her horse, practising jumping down by the river. Mr Charlton was watching her. Ma called from the house that lunch was ready. Pop looked up at the midday sun and the clear, blue sky.

'Perfick,' he thought. 'It's going to be a wonderful afternoon.'

♦

All afternoon Mr Charlton watched Mariette riding and jumping in the gymkhana. She looked wonderful on her horse. He was happier than ever before in his life.

Ma was happy, too. Only Mariette and Montgomery were riding, but all the children were dressed in riding trousers, jackets and hats. They walked around the field eating large ice-creams or bags of sweets. They watched the activities and had fun with their friends. Ma was dressed beautifully, in a pale blue dress and shoes. She wore a large, dark blue hat to keep the sun off her face.

The Brigadier's sister was there, looking thin and pale next to Ma.

'Are you riding in this ladies' donkey race?' Ma asked her.

The Brigadier's sister shook her head, unamused by the idea.

'I think Miss Pilchester's doing it. Pop's going to ask her,' said Ma. 'He thinks she'll be good at it. He's got a silver cup for the winner.'

Behind the beer tent, Pop was trying to make Miss Pilchester agree to the idea.

'I really couldn't. It will be just terrible.'

'I thought you liked a bit of fun?'

Miss Pilchester looked at Pop. She thought he looked more handsome than ever that afternoon. He was wearing a brown checked suit, an orange tie and a new brown hat. His eyes were bright and he had a big smile on his face.

'I just need one more rider and then we'll have seven. Please, Edith. For me.'

'Who are the other riders?'

'All girls of your age,' said Pop.

This wasn't true. Miss Pilchester was about forty. The other riders were all much younger than her.

'Now you're being silly.'

Pop tried again.

'Remember that time I took you home in the Rolls?'

Miss Pilchester couldn't forget it.

'What about it?'

'It was the best kiss I've had for a long time,' said Pop. 'Beautiful! I haven't forgotten it. Are you coming to the cocktail party?'

'Yes, I am.'

'We could repeat that kiss tonight at the cocktail party. I promise!' said Pop.

♦

At four o'clock, Miss Pilchester was ready to ride in the ladies' donkey race. First, there was a race for the men. Montgomery and Mr Charlton both rode in the men's donkey race, and most of the donkeys didn't want to start running at all. Mr Charlton's donkey was called Jasmine and he soon fell off her.

Jasmine ran away from the gymkhana field and down to the river. When Pop found her, she was watching a young man and his girlfriend. They were lying together in the long grass. They didn't see Jasmine because they were kissing. She was very interested in them and didn't want to go back to the field. It was difficult for Pop to make her move. He decided that Jasmine was the perfect donkey for Miss Pilchester to ride.

At the start of the ladies' race, Jasmine stood very quietly. She didn't move. Pop told Miss Pilchester what to do.

'Hold tight with your knees.'

Miss Pilchester was afraid of falling off the donkey. She looked around at the other riders. She was surprised that they were all girls of sixteen or seventeen.

'Don't worry about them, Edith,' said Pop. 'Just hold on tight. Try to go as straight as you can.'

Some of the other donkeys started slowly. Some moved a few steps and then stopped. Some didn't move at all.

Jasmine stood with her head down, eating grass. Pop pushed her from behind. She didn't move. He hit her bottom. She still didn't move. Pop pushed again, but it was no good. Jasmine didn't want to race.

Suddenly, there was a sound from one of the microphones and Jasmine lifted her head. She immediately started running and Pop fell onto the ground behind her. Miss Pilchester held on tight, and together they ran across the field and away from the gymkhana.

In less than a minute Jasmine was back at her favourite place – the river.

The young man and his girlfriend were in the same place. Jasmine saw them, stopped suddenly, and Miss Pilchester fell off. She landed next to the young man. He looked at her, and then he looked up at Jasmine.

'Why don't you two go away?' he asked. 'Both of you. You *and* your sister.'

Chapter 7 Surprises at Pop's Party

The gymkhana was a great success. Pop spent most of the afternoon saying hello to people. Some he knew and some he didn't know. He couldn't remember who exactly was invited to the party. He said the same thing to everyone.

'See you at eight o'clock. See you at the party.'

The result was that by half past eight the house was full of people – about fifty or sixty of them.

'I don't think we invited so many people,' said Ma. 'Will we have enough food for everyone?'

A big table was covered with the food, champagne and glasses. Pop and Ma, helped by Mariette, Mr Charlton and Montgomery, took plates of food to people and poured champagne.

Now and then, someone came up to Pop and said, 'Wonderful party, Larkin. Well done.'

Suddenly, Pop found the two Miss Barnwells – quiet, shy little ladies from the village. To his surprise, they didn't have any food or glasses of champagne.

'Nothing to eat? Nothing to drink?'

'Please don't worry about us,' said one of the Miss Barnwells. 'We just like to see so many people enjoying themselves.'

'I'll get you some champagne,' said Pop.

'No, no,' they said together. 'Nothing like that.'

'Then I'll get you some sandwiches.'

He came back very soon with some of Ma's chicken sandwiches. He was still a little unhappy because they had nothing to drink.

'Glass of beer? Glass of wine?' he asked again.

'No, no, we're quite happy.'

'Have a My Darling.'

The Miss Barnwells became interested.

'What is a My Darling?'

Pop thought quickly. It wasn't a strong cocktail like the Rolls Royce, or the Driver. In his opinion it was quite weak and uninteresting. Maybe, he thought, it was something they would like.

'Mostly fruit juice,' he said.

'That sounds quite nice. Perhaps we could have two of those.'

Pop went away and mixed two My Darling cocktails. They didn't look very exciting, so he added a little whisky to each.

'There you are,' he said, giving a glass to each of the ladies. 'I'll bring you another one soon.'

A few minutes later, a hand pulled at his arm. He turned around and saw a tall lady in a small grey hat.

'Mr Larkin,' she said, smiling over her glass of champagne. 'Lady Bluff-Gore. You remember?'

'Ah, yes,' Pop said. 'Lady Rose.'

'We don't meet very often,' she said.

'Not often enough,' said Pop.

'I understand you suggested something quite interesting to my husband this afternoon.'

'Oh! About the house? That's right. It's time it was pulled down.'

'That's what I heard.'

Lady Rose thought it was an interesting idea. She also wanted to pull Bluff Court down.

'Who wants these old places?' Pop asked.

She agreed. There were miles of stables that weren't used. There were gardens that nobody looked after. Worst of all, there was that big, cold house they didn't live in. Better to have some money in the bank, she thought.

'How much money were you thinking of?' she asked Pop.

'I can come over and look at it tomorrow,' he replied.

'Do you think we could talk somewhere a little more … private? There are so many people here.'

They walked into the garden. A few other people were also there getting some air. It was a warm, cloudy evening and rain was on its way. Pop guided Lady Rose to the tree by the kitchen door so they could be alone.

'My husband doesn't like the idea,' Lady Rose said. 'It won't be easy to change his mind.'

'No?'

'Not an easy man.'

Pop believed her.

'But I think I can do it. Then perhaps a small amount of the money can come straight to me. No need for my husband to know anything about this.'

Pop understood. 'Clever,' he thought. 'Women are clever.'

'I'm sure that will be fine,' he said.

'I'll need some time. Shall I let you know when we'll need another little talk?'

Back in the house, Pop discovered the Miss Barnwells, both with empty glasses. They looked happy and their faces were quite red.

'Did you like the My Darlings?' he asked. 'I'll get you some more.'

Pop went to the living room and mixed the two cocktails. It was quieter in there, away from all the people.

'And what about me?' said a woman's voice behind him.

It was Miss Pilchester.

'Are you having a nice time?' Pop asked her.

'It'll be nicer when you keep your promise,' she replied.

Pop put down the two glasses and took Miss Pilchester into his arms. Pop preferred kissing Ma, and he didn't enjoy it much. But a promise was a promise.

'Thanks,' said Miss Pilchester. 'Time for another one?'

'Just one more, then I must get back to the party.'

As he kissed her, Pop was thinking about the fireworks. Maybe one or two? There were no more horses in the field.

'I just want to say that it's all been wonderful,' said Miss Pilchester. 'The gymkhana was the best we've ever had, and now this party ... You've made me very happy.'

Miss Pilchester hurried away, and Pop went back to the Miss Barnwells with their drinks. They were laughing, and eating more sandwiches and cheese.

'Can we talk, just for a few minutes?'

The voice came from behind Pop. At the same time, a hand

reached out and touched his shoulder. He turned and saw a beautiful young lady with long, fair hair and large, green eyes. He didn't know her.

'They tell me you planned this day almost alone. Wonderful. What a success! And now this party.'

Pop looked at her. Unusually, he couldn't think of anything to say. Her dress was pale yellow, with a low neck. Her skin was almost white.

'I'm going to have a party, too. Please say you'll come.'

'Well … yes … I'd like that …'

'That donkey race – they say it was your idea.'

Pop agreed that it was. He felt quite proud of it.

'It was just what the gymkhana needed. I laughed and laughed! So funny! Excellent idea,' she said, laughing again at the thought of it. 'Now, dear man. My name's Angela Snow, from Emhurst Valley. We've got one of these boring gymkhanas in August – why don't you come over and bring the donkeys?'

She held on to Pop's hand.

Pop started to think that he and Angela Snow thought the same way. Maybe they also enjoyed the same things. Suddenly, he remembered the fireworks.

'Do you like fireworks?'

'I love them!'

'Wait here,' said Pop. 'I'll get you some more champagne. Or maybe you'd prefer a cocktail?'

'I love cocktails!'

'Then come this way.'

Pop and Angela Snow were almost at the living room door when Mr Charlton and Mariette found them.

'Pop, Charley has something he'd like to say to you.'

'Not now, I'm busy,' said Pop.

'It's very important. It's something he's got to ask you.'

'I'll be back in five minutes.'

In the living room, Pop told Angela Snow about his cocktails.

'Which one would you like? The Rolls Royce is the strongest,' he said.

'Then I'll have a Rolls Royce,' she replied.

Pop mixed two Rolls Royce cocktails and Angela Snow drank hers quickly.

'One more of these, and I'm ready,' she said.

Pop was ready, too. Ten minutes later, the first firework went off under Ma. She wasn't at all worried by it. Pop put fireworks on the stairs and Angela Snow put two small ones under the Brigadier's sister. Then she put another under Sir George Bluff-Gore.

Ma started laughing. The Miss Barnwells laughed, too.

Miss Pilchester said, 'This is just terrible,' and hid under the stairs.

People started running from the house into the garden. Pop had more fireworks there. Upstairs, the young Larkin children looked out of the windows and laughed at the adults.

Miss Pilchester came out into the garden. She thought it was safer there. Pop put a firework under her. She screamed and ran back into the house.

Pop ran around the garden with a firework and finally threw it into the yard. It was a shower of silver and pink stars.

Mr Charlton found him by the stables.

'Pop, I want to speak to you. Can I marry Mariette? Ma says it's OK. But only if you say yes.'

'Perfick! Marry her? Of course you can marry her!'

'Will you tell everyone now? Ma thinks it's the perfect time.'

A quarter of an hour later, Pop was standing on a chair in the house. He told all the guests about the wedding plans of Mr Charlton and his daughter Mariette. Everyone filled their glasses.

'To Charley and Mariette!' he called.

As he lifted his glass, Angela Snow threw the last firework

Pop and Ma with Mariette and her future husband

towards him. There was a loud noise. The firework knocked Pop over the back of the chair and Ma laughed and laughed.

'Quite perfect,' said Angela Snow.

◆

When the television was finished for the night, Ma and Pop sat alone in the kitchen. Ma kept laughing. She was thinking about the donkeys, Miss Pilchester and the last firework.

'Nothing to eat?' asked Pop.

'There's a fruit cake,' said Ma, and she put it on the table with two plates and a knife.

'Who was that girl in the yellow dress?' she asked.

'I've never seen her before,' said Pop. 'I think her father's a judge.'

Pop cut two large pieces of cake, then found a bottle of red wine and poured out two glasses.

'Where are Charley and Mariette?' he asked Ma.

'They're having a quiet few minutes in the living room.' Ma looked down at the rings on her large, fat fingers. 'And while we're alone, I want to tell you something. We're going to have another baby.'

Pop looked surprised, but not unhappy.

'When did that happen?'

'That evening just before Mr Charlton arrived. We went to the woods to hear the nightingale.'

'Oh, yes. I remember.' Pop took her hand. 'Well, here's an idea for you. What do you think about us getting married at the same time as Mariette and Charley? A double wedding.'

'That's a good idea,' said Ma. 'Why not?'

They sat in silence for a few minutes. Pop was thinking about the new baby. Ma was thinking about his surprising suggestion of getting married.

'Thought of any names for it?' Pop asked.

'I've got a feeling it's going to be *them*, not *it*,' said Ma. 'I like Lucinda and Clorinda, if they're girls. Or if they're boys, Nelson and Rodney. What do you think?'

'I like Lucinda,' said Pop.

Outside it was raining softly, and there was still a smell of firework smoke in the air. They listened to the rain until Ma said,

'We'll ask Charley about having a double wedding. He'll know how to do it. He knows a lot of things – he was very clever about the cocktail party.'

Pop was just finishing his second piece of fruit cake when Mr Charlton and Mariette came into the kitchen.

'Now it's quieter, I want to say something. Ma and I are very pleased about you two,' he said. 'How about a glass of wine?'

He poured two more glasses, then he kissed Mariette and shook Mr Charlton's hand. Ma kissed them both.

'And we've got a bit of news of our own,' Pop said. 'We've decided to get married, too. Ma's going to have another baby.'

Mr Charlton and Mariette didn't look surprised by this. Mr Charlton drank a little of his wine. He thought that this was a good time to use his head.

'Now wait a minute,' he said. 'This needs thinking about.'

'Why?' asked Ma. 'What is there to think about?'

'The tax problem,' said Mr Charlton. 'One day, you will have to pay a tax bill. It will be lower if you're not married. You'll pay less tax.'

Pop was silent for a minute. 'Well, we're quite happy as we are. Aren't we, Ma?' he said.

'I think so. Let's just continue in the old sweet way,' said Ma. 'Oh! I wanted to ask you, Charley – are you going back to that office?'

He thought for a minute.

'I'm not sure,' he said, finally.

'Use your head, Charley,' said Pop. 'I'm going to pull down an old house near here quite soon – it'll be a big job. You and I can save the best bits and build you and Mariette a nice little house down by the wood. What do you say?'

Mariette ran to Pop and kissed him.

'It'll be wonderful!' she cried.

Mr Charlton watched her. There was really nothing more to say.

'Perfick. Now, one more drink before bed?'

Pop took his glass of wine to the kitchen door and looked out at the summer night and the rain. Mr Charlton joined him. He thought back to the spring, now in the past. The buds of May were flowers, and now it was summer.

'Listen,' Pop said. 'Perfick.'

They all listened, and in the dark air there was the sound of nightingales.

ACTIVITIES

Chapter 1

Before you read

1 Find out what England is like in May. Which of these can you usually see or hear?

   a flowering trees

   b snow

   c bird song

   d sunshine

   e blue skies

2 Look at the Word List at the back of the book. Which are words …

   a for food and drink?

   b for birds and animals?

   c of interest to horse riders?

   d for money that many people don't like paying?

While you read

3 Who says these words?

   a 'Where's Mariette? Isn't she there?'

   b 'There's a man in the yard.'

   c 'You haven't sent us your tax form.'

   d 'Three minutes, or I'll give it to the cats.'

   e 'You spend too much time in that office.'

   f 'If we stand by this gate, we can listen to the birds.'

   g 'A few days like this and those strawberries will be ready to pick.'

After you read

4 Answer these questions.

   What:

   a is in the Larkins' yard?

   b is in Mr Charlton's black case?

   c are the Larkins having for dinner?

   Why:

   d can't Mr Charlton speak when he sees Mariette?

   e does he know her face?

   f does Pop invite Mr Charlton to dinner?

Who:

g takes a pen from his pocket?

h goes to the woods?

i burns the tax form?

5 Mr Charlton joins the Larkins for dinner. Which of these does he eat?

a	chocolate cake	**e**	bread and butter
b	ice-cream	**f**	fruit
c	boiled eggs	**g**	goose
d	fish and chips	**h**	chicken

6 Work with another student.

Student A: You are Mariette. Tell Mr Charlton about your family.

Student B: You are Mr Charlton. Tell Mariette what surprises you about the Larkins' life.

Chapter 2

Before you read

7 Discuss these questions. What do you think?

a Will Mr Charlton visit the Larkins again?

b Will Pop fill in a tax form?

c Will Mr Charlton fall in love with Mariette?

While you read

8 Number these sentences in the right order, 1–6.

a Ma cooks steaks. .....

b Mr Charlton tries to understand the card game. .....

c Mariette puts on some of Ma's perfume. .....

d Pop mixes Rolls Royce cocktails. .....

e Mariette finds some pyjamas for Mr Charlton. .....

f Pop feeds the pigs. .....

After you read

9 Answer these questions.

a What does Montgomery say will happen on Monday?

b Why doesn't Mr Charlton catch the eight o'clock bus?

c What does Pop add to the cups of tea?

d What is Mariette's perfume called?

e What does Pop use to mix the Driver cocktail?

51

10 Discuss what Mr Charlton thinks of

    a the card game.   **d** Mariette.

    b the cocktails.   **e** Pop and Ma.

    c the food.

11 Why does Pop ask Ma about Mr Charlton at the end of the chapter? Why does she think he needs a little more time?

Chapter 3

Before you read

12 How do you think Mr Charlton feels the next morning? Do you think he will remember the tax form?

While you read

13 Are these sentences right (✔) or wrong (✗)?

    a There is a lot of noise outside Mr Charlton's bedroom window.   .....

    b Mr Charlton has two eggs for breakfast.   .....

    c Pop mixes him a Larkin Special.   .....

    d Mr Charlton wants to get back to the office.   .....

    e The Larkin Special makes him feel better.   .....

14 Circle the correct word.

    a Ma cooked the geese for *lunch / dinner*.

    b The Brigadier lives *near / far away from* the Larkins.

    c There is a problem with the *judge / field* for the gymkhana.

    d Pop wants to have *music / fireworks* after the gymkhana.

    e Mariette and Mr Charlton run towards the *village / river*.

After you read

15 Who is speaking?

    a 'Two eggs or three?'

    b 'Can we call you Charley?'

    c 'Do you know what happened to that tax form?'

    d 'It's like riding on air.'

    e 'I've got a bit of a problem.'

    f 'What wrong with them?'

    g 'You're a lovely, lovely man.'

16 Mr Charlton decides to stay with the Larkins for another day. Why? How is he changing?

Chapter 4

Before you read

17 What do you think is going to happen next? Choose the best answer(s).

    a Mr Charlton goes back to his office.

    b Mr Charlton stays with the Larkins.

    c Mariette says he should stay longer.

    d Ma says he should go home.

18 Have you ever been strawberry picking? Do you think it is easy or hard work? Why?

While you read

19 Put these words in the right sentences. Use each word only once.

    tent   strawberries   weight   sings   check   ache

    a Pop says Mr Charlton will have back .... that night.

    b Everyone in the lorry ...., but Mr Charlton stays silent.

    c Mr Charlton doesn't want to eat any ....

    d They take the boxes of fruit to the ....

    e Mr Charlton writes down the .... of the boxes.

    f He has to .... every box.

20 Why

    a does Mariette fight with Pauline Jackson?

    b does Mr Charlton think the two girls are hurt?

    c does he stop worrying about the strawberry tax?

    d does Ma decide not to hurry with the cooking?

After you read

21 Work with another student. Talk about the fight in the strawberry field. Decide who won the fight!

    Student A: You are a friend of Mariette's.

    Student B: You are a friend of Pauline Jackson's.

22 Why do you think Mr Charlton asks Pop about the strawberry tax? Do you think he will tell his office about the women picking strawberries? Why (not)?

Chapter 5

Before you read

23 Look at the title of this chapter.
  a Can you remember who Miss Pilchester is?
  b How is she important in the village?
  c Who do you think kisses her?

While you read

24 Who is Pop speaking to when he says:
  a 'The field is all yours. You can come and go at any time.'
  b 'We'll ask him to have a look at Charley.'
  c 'You can speak into this pipe and give me orders.'
  d 'It was a bit like kissing a horse.'

After you read

25 Complete these sentences.
  a Miss Pilchester lived alone and had no help ...
  b In her mind Miss Pilchester could already see the field ...
  c She still remembered a kiss at a village dance ...
  d As usual in the Larkins' house ...
  e Pop turned the sound down ...

  1) but he didn't turn the television off.
  2) a year or more ago.
  3) with her house or garden.
  4) the television was on.
  5) on gymkhana day.

26 Is Mr Charlton being dishonest about his back ache? Would you do the same? Why (not)?

27 Why isn't Ma worried about Pop kissing Miss Pilchester?

Chapter 6

Before you read

28 What do you think is going to happen to these people at the gymkhana?

a	Mariette	**c**	Mr Charlton
b	Miss Pilchester	**d**	Pop

While you read

29 Where do these happen?

    a The judge waits for Edith.   ....

    b Pop talks to Sir George Bluff.   ....

    c Rosemary Bluff is taking an art course.   ....

    d Mariette and her horse practise jumping. ....

    e Pop talks to Miss Pilchester about the

        donkey race.   ....

    f Jasmine finds a young man kissing his girlfriend. ....

After you read

30 On the day of the gymkhana, which of the Larkins is wearing these clothes?

a	a dark blue hat	**e**	a brown hat
b	a brown checked jacket	**f**	an orange tie
c	dark green trousers	**g**	a pale yellow shirt
d	a pale blue dress	**h**	riding trousers, jackets and hats

31 Complete these sentences with the right numbers.

    a Pop needs … riders in the donkey race.

    b Miss Pilchester is about … years old.

    c The men's donkey race is at ... o'clock.

    d The other riders in the ladies' race are … or … years old.

    e It takes Jasmine less than … minute to get back to the river.

32 Work with another student. Have this conversation.

    Student A: You are the judge. You have just arrived at the gymkhana field. Ask Miss Pilchester about the gymkhana.

    Student B: You are Miss Pilchester. Tell the judge about the plans for the day. Explain whose field you are using, and why.

Chapter 7

Before you read

33 What surprises do you think Pop has for the party?

34 Do you think there will be surprises from other people at the party? What do you think they will be?

While you read

35 Circle the correct names.

    a Lady Rose says that *the Brigadier / Sir George / Mr Charlton* is not an easy man.

    b Pop kisses *Miss Barnwell / Lady Rose / Miss Pilchester.*

    c *Lady Rose / Miss Pilchester / Angela Snow* loves fireworks and cocktails.

    d *Sir George / Charley / The Brigadier* has something very important to say to Pop.

    e The first firework goes off under *Mariette / Ma / the Brigadier's sister.*

    f *Ma / Miss Pilchester / Miss Barnwell* hides under the stairs.

    g *Mr Charlton finds Sir George / the Brigadier / Pop* by the stables.

    h The last firework goes off under *Mr Charlton / Pop / Sir George.*

After you read

36 Pop and Lady Rose Bluff-Gore have a little talk at the party. Correct this description of their conversation.

Lady Rose Bluff-Gore is a short lady in a blue hat. She and Pop meet quite often in the village. She doesn't like Pop's idea of pulling down Bluff Court. She wants to live in the house because it's big and comfortable. Pop wants to look at the house next week. They walk in the garden together. Nobody is there, so they can talk in private. Lady Rose thinks that Sir George likes Pop's idea. She isn't interested in getting any money from the house. Pop thinks she is a clever lady.

37 The fireworks are Pop's surprise on the night of the party.

    a What is Charley's surprise?

    b What is Ma's surprise?

38 Pop wants a double wedding. Explain why Charley doesn't think it is a good idea.

39 Discuss which words best describe Pop Larkin.
amusing happy sad nervous friendly clever ordinary
romantic ugly boring

Writing

40 Write a description of the Larkins' home. Write about their house, yard and garden.

41 Imagine that you are Mr Charlton's boss. You call him into your office before the story begins. You explain why he must see Pop Larkin. You tell him what he must do there. Write your speech.

42 Imagine a usual day with the Larkins. Write a list of their meals for the day. What do they eat and drink, and when?

43 Imagine that you are Mr Charlton. Write about your first Sunday with the Larkins. Start like this: *I woke up with a terrible headache. I went down to the kitchen for breakfast …*

44 The Larkins invite you to go strawberry picking with them. Write a letter to a friend. Tell him/her about your day in the strawberry fields.

45 Imagine that you are Mr Charlton. Write your letter to the tax office. Explain why you can't go to work. Don't give the real reasons!

46 Write a report for the local newspaper about the gymkhana. Who are the important people there? Who wins some of the races? Write about the two donkey races.

47 Write a conversation between the Brigadier, his sister and Miss Pilchester. The cocktail party has ended and they are walking home together. What does each person think about the gymkhana and the party?

48 It is now a year after the story ends. What is different in the lives of the Larkins?

49 Which person in the book do you like best? Why? What is your favourite part of the story?

WORD LIST

brigadier (n) an important British soldier

bud (n) a young flower before it opens

chips (n pl) long, thin pieces of potato cooked in very hot oil

champagne (n) an expensive French white wine for special parties

cocktail (n) a strong drink made by mixing different drinks together, often with fruit

darling (n) someone or something that is much loved

donkey (n) a grey or brown animal like a small horse with long ears

firework (n) something that makes coloured lights and loud noises in the sky

goose (n, pl **geese**) a large farm bird, usually white with a long neck

gymkhana (n) horse riding and jumping watched by a lot of people

kid (n) another word for 'child'

nightingale (n) a small bird that sings beautifully

perfume (n) something with a strong, pleasant smell that women put on their body

pyjamas (n pl) light trousers and a shirt that you wear in bed

spin (v) to turn round and round very quickly

stable (n) a building where horses are kept

strawberry (n) a summer fruit that is small, red and sweet

tax (n) money that everyone has to pay to the government

whisky (n) a strong drink, stronger than beer or wine, that is made in Scotland and Ireland, for example

yard (n) a hard area of ground outside a house or farm